Seeing &
Believing

Reflections for Faith

A Devotional Journal

Photographs and Text by
Robert Boak Slocum

WIPF & STOCK · Eugene, Oregon

Wipf and Stock Publishers
199 W 8th Ave, Suite 3
Eugene, OR 97401

Seeing & Believing
Reflections for Faith, A Devotional Journal
By Slocum, Robert Boak
Copyright©2013 by Slocum, Robert Boak
ISBN 13: 978-1-5326-6364-2
Publication date 1/1/2019
Previously published by Forward Movement, 2013

Dedication

I dedicate this book to all the amazing people who provide daily images and reminders of God's glory, including those mentioned in these pages, especially Victoria, Claire, Rebecca, and Jacob. I also dedicate this book to John Graves, a student in my "Explorations of Theology" class at Saint Catharine College, who encouraged this project from the beginning.

Introduction

This collection of images and meditations provides a starting point for reflections of faith. New faith calls for new images of faith. We may discover images that speak deeply to us, beyond our understanding, allowing us to experience and share more fully the truths we know but can't quite put into words. These images can be "snapshots" of meaning for us. Our imagination is especially a place of grace where God meets us and we meet God. Images of faith can stir our imagination, renewing and transforming us. Even a glimpse of transcendence can change us. Imagination connects our everyday life to the transcendent and holy beyond ourselves.

Images can also provide a way of sharing faith and deepening theological understanding. We can "do theology" through images and the reflections prompted by them. It's a way of knowing. We may discover that some images touch us deeply, engaging us in ways we can't explain and helping us know the truths that the images make visible. And we may share these images with others to help them see insights or to share an understanding that could be difficult to relate in other ways.

Each image in this collection is followed by a reflection, and then questions to encourage active imagination and connect the image to personal experience. Each set extends an invitation to deeper seeing and believing.

Let these images and reflections stir up new ideas and ways of being. Write your thoughts and prayers in response to the pictures and words. Draw your own images on the blank pages in the back of the journal. Keep your own snapshots, drawings, or special reminders in the folder at the back. You may use these reflections on a weekly basis or as a resource during a liturgical season or a time of your life. You determine how this collection may best strengthen your journey. I hope these images and words will reflect the "gracious light" among us, and assist your seeing and believing. — *Rob Slocum*

Lord, we love thee, always be
in our hearts and minds to see
all our gifts have come from thee.
Lord, we love thee, help us see.

Lord, we love thee, nearer be
never let us fail to see
every day we walk with thee.
Lord, we love thee, help us see.

Lord, we love thee,
constantly
filling all our hearts to see
life and hope will come from thee.
Lord, we love thee, help us see.

— RBS

Arrows

One summer our church hosted Reading Camp, a week-long event for third and fourth graders in the local area. It met in the parish hall, behind the church, so Victoria, my wife as well as the camp director, chalked large blue arrows on sidewalk squares, all leading to the parish hall. The arrows helped the kids find their way to where they were going. Later that week, there was a torrential rain, and it washed away all the arrows, without a trace.

But the camp went on. By then, everyone knew the way. The arrows were gone, but their direction was still with us. It was a busy and great camp. And I was tired after we finished on the last day. That night I went to bed early, and in my own twilight between sleeping and waking, I could almost hear the sounds of the kids' voices one more time. Then I woke up completely and found myself in a darkened room that was absolutely quiet. But the life of the camp and the kids' voices were inside me. The outward sign was gone, but its energy remained. In me.

Everything we do in the church is meant to point beyond itself to something more. Nothing is for its own sake—not the fellowship, or the organization, or the budget, or the liturgy, or the building. They're all arrows that point beyond themselves. They point to love that will be with us when all the arrows are gone.

Do you see the arrows? Where do they point you? How do you feel when they disappear? What's your direction now? What will you do?

Monkey Trap

Some trappers in South America seek to capture monkeys without harming them, to take them to zoos and such. So they take a large gourd and empty it on the inside, much as we might empty out a pumpkin to make a jack-o-lantern at Halloween. They carve a small hole in the side of the gourd, making an opening that's just big enough for the monkey's paw. Inside, they place some tasty nuts that the monkey will love to eat and then secure the trap. When the monkey arrives, he slips his paw into the gourd, and it just fits. But when he closes his paw on the nuts, he's trapped! Of course, the monkey can leave at any time. All he has to do is let go of the nuts, and he's free to go. But he doesn't want to do that! He wants the nuts. So he'll stay there with his paw in the gourd until the trappers arrive to take him away.

Sometimes we trap ourselves by our unwillingness to let go. We get stuck and can't take the next steps. We hold on to something that's really gone, unavailable, or inappropriate—maybe it's a time of life, a way of thinking, or an ended relationship. We tie ourselves down in ways that prevent us from living the life that's available right now. No amount of discussion or explanation will really make a difference. We just need to let go and move on.

If your hand isn't open, you can't receive a gift. There's no room if your hands are full. If your hand is closed, you may turn away a friend or someone who could be a friend. And certainly, as Indira Gandhi says, you can't shake hands with a clenched fist.

If you look at your hand, what do you see? Is it closed, like a fist? Are you holding on, clutching at something? Are you full? Are you stuck? Are you trapped? Or is your hand open for all you can receive?

The Pearl

The Gospel of Matthew records a parable of the kingdom of God: it's like a merchant in search of fine pearls who sold everything to buy one amazing pearl. In a related parable, also in Matthew, a man joyfully sells everything he has to buy a field where treasure is hidden.

Our first priority is the kingdom of God, whatever the cost. As author T. S. Eliot writes in the *Four Quartets*, our completion and fulfillment is a condition of complete simplicity, costing not less than everything. The great pearl surpasses everything. It's peerless and priceless. God offers everything and invites us to give everything in return. And we're most ourselves when we offer back everything. We may be amazed to see all we can give.

The buyer of pearls can count himself lucky to find the great one. The enormous price is not a burden or a grudging duty. It's an amazing bargain. This great discovery calls for a complete response, with no holding back or compromise. Nothing less will do. As Saint Augustine says, our hearts are restless until they rest in God. The pearl, the treasure, the kingdom of God is worth every sacrifice, every price, everything.

What's your pearl? Where do you find it? How do you claim it? What does it cost you? What do you give?

The Clouds and the Mountain

I once visited friends in Oregon who said they lived near Mount Hood. "It's that way," they said, pointing toward the large window that faced the backyard. But the view showed only an overcast of clouds and fog, and that's all I saw for days. Then the weather cleared, and I saw the majesty of Mount Hood in the far distance beyond the house. Of course, the mountain was there all along, even when I couldn't see it.

Jesus' divinity was manifested in a dramatic way when he was transfigured on a high mountain before Peter, James, and John (Mark 9:2-8). His clothes became dazzling white. Moses and Elijah appeared and talked with him. Peter urged the disciples to make dwellings for Jesus, Moses, and Elijah, perhaps seeing Jesus as their equal. This was not a helpful suggestion. The disciples were terrified by Jesus' transfiguration, and they really didn't know what to say. It was awe-full. A cloud overshadowed them, and a voice from the cloud said, "This is my Son, the Beloved; listen to him!"

Peter, James, and John may well have seen Jesus in a new light after the Transfiguration. But it's important to remember the Transfiguration added nothing to Jesus' divinity. He was the incarnate Son of God when he approached the mountain of the Transfiguration, and the incarnate Son of God when he left that place. His being and identity were unchanged. But something was different. Jesus was clearly and powerfully manifested to his closest followers, making it possible for them to see the truth about him. His glory was revealed in a moment for them to see. It was as if the overcast finally cleared, disclosing the beautiful mountain that had been concealed from their sight and understanding. Finally they saw him.

The mountain was present whether I saw it or not. Jesus is the Son of God, whether I believe the story or not. I saw the mountain, but not when I first looked. I saw it, but not when I expected.

Can you see the beautiful mountain? How do you feel when the overcast clears and the mountain appears? When have you been amazed by a beautiful moment? What did you see?

Gathered Fragments

After the miraculous feeding of the five thousand, Jesus tells his followers to gather up the fragments left over from the five barley loaves and two fish, "so that nothing may be lost" (John 6:12). James DeKoven, a controversial Episcopal priest in the 1800s, preached one of his last sermons on this passage, reflecting that only in God are the broken fragments of our lives to be gathered up and made whole. DeKoven could well have felt his own life was fragmented. He was elected to be bishop of Illinois, but concerns about his theology prevented him from receiving the necessary consents for his election. Many people opposed him. And yet he pointed to an integration and wholeness of life that surpassed the limits of his own story.

Gather up the fragments! The miracle is visible in every piece that remains when the five thousand have eaten. Gather the fragments! That's a prayer for the broken pieces in our lives and the love of God that's present. Gather the hurts, the disappointments, and the missed opportunities. Gather the possibilities that could have been, and the relationships that were lost. Gather the things that were badly used or never tried. Gather all the shards and broken pieces. Gather everyone left standing when the music stopped. Gather us all into a greater whole, with divine hands more capable than our own. Gather the fragments.

What are the fragments of your life? Are the fragments sharp and painful, or smooth and well worn? Do they fit together readily like puzzle pieces, or are they broken like shards? Can you offer your fragments as a gift? What brings them together?

Fast Forward

Once when I was serving at a large parish, I went to the media center with another staff member to watch a video about parish life. We put the video on "fast forward" to find a particular segment for an upcoming program. As I watched the television screen, images from parish life flickered by at many times normal speed. Meetings were held, hospitality was offered, pastoral conversations were shared, a Christmas pageant unfolded, communion was distributed—all at lightning speed.

I watched with fascination and horror. The fast forward mode created a distortion of the parish life video, but it also showed the truth of parish life. Everything we did there was on "double time." Life and ministry were hectic, stressed, and fast. The story of our parish would have been written in italics, with exclamation points! We did everything, and, in a sense, we did everything really well—except breathe. Fast forward didn't work as a way of life or ministry. It's hard to draw people to the heart of faith when a hyperactive schedule pulls everything off center.

There are times when we need to rest. A rest in a musical composition doesn't mean the piece is over or lacking energy. The rest is part of the musical composition and its beauty. It is a momentary pause that allows the musical themes to come together more beautifully.

Jesus invites us to rest. We may recall Jesus' words of invitation: "Come to me, all you that are weary and are carrying heavy burdens, and I will give you rest" (Matthew 11:28). In a similar way, after the execution of John the Baptist, the apostles gathered around Jesus and told him "all that they had done and taught." It was a busy time: "many were coming and going, and they had no leisure even to eat." Jesus said to them, "Come away to a deserted place all by yourselves and rest a while" (Mark 6:30-31). He never asked them to be hyperactive. He asked them to be people of faith who were centered, whole, and generous. He shares that invitation with us and offers times of rest.

Do you ever get stuck on fast forward? What happens? How do you feel? Does that change how you treat others, and yourself? How do you rest? Is there a place or time for you to rest? When? How is life different when you're rested?

Sirens

My first home parish, Saint Paul's Episcopal Church in Macon, Georgia, was a few blocks from the main hospital and emergency room in the city. The church was located near the street, and it was not unusual for the sermon or eucharistic prayer to be interrupted by the sounds of an ambulance rushing by with its siren roaring. This may have been the occasion for some people to offer a silent prayer for the patient going to the hospital, while others just waited for the siren to pass and the noise to end. Either way, the problem was outside and passing. It involved someone else. It was their problem, which might or might not be viewed with compassion.

In the 500s, Saint Benedict encourages his monks to find Christ in the community member who is sick. As Jesus says, help given to the most needy of his brothers and sisters is help given to him (Matthew 25:40). This service is not a reluctant duty endured for the sake of principle. We find Christ as we extend radical hospitality to help the sick, disoriented, or impoverished. Their need is not just someone else's problem. It's not even just a problem. It's life and salvation. As we help others, we discover Christ's love present—and we uncover our true selves. We're connected with others in love, and their problems are ours.

During a time of plague in England, John Donne, an Anglican priest and writer, warned against asking for whom the death bell tolls, because it tolls "for thee," for each of us. Today the sirens ring for us, as we hear the sounds of suffering and distress in our own communities, calling us to serve.

Can you hear the siren outside? How do you respond? How do you feel? What can you offer? What will you do? Have you seen Jesus in a person who needed your help?

Lost in the Dark

I once spent the night in a friend's house in Nashville, Tennessee, and I thought I knew the place pretty well. The house was very dark, and I needed to get to the opposite corner of the room. No problem, I thought, I can find my way without turning on lights and disturbing everybody. So I started toward the door. After a few confident steps, I discovered that solid objects were not where I expected. I was not where I expected. The door on the other side of the room was not where I expected. So I thought I would return to my starting point. Unfortunately, the way back was as obscure as the way out. Nothing was where it belonged. I wasn't even sure where to find the walls, so I couldn't feel for the light switch. I knew the room, but I couldn't see it in the dark. I was lost!

My vision was fine, but I couldn't see. My eyes would have been able to see with adequate light, but I was lost in the dark. I really thought I could find my way across that room in the pitch dark, but I was wrong.

Sometimes we talk about our sight as if it were an independent power of our own. Someone might say, "I have 20/20 vision," but it's really just potential, a capacity to see under the right conditions. In dim light we cannot see well, and in true darkness our eyes are useless.

In the Gospel of John, Jesus heals a man who was born blind, but the Pharisees can't see the miracle. They're blinded by certainty that Jesus is a sinner who couldn't possibly open the eyes of a person born without sight. After the miracle that opens the eyes of the blind man, he finds himself in a confrontation with disbelieving Pharisees. He tells them the truth of what he's seen, but they can't accept it. They drive him out. Their eyes see, but they're blind. They close their eyes to unexpected light. They won't see beyond themselves, and so they can't. They reject the truth because it doesn't fit their preconceptions and prejudices. Refusal to see is the most dangerous blindness.

The light we need to live is a gift. If we imagine we stand alone, or act on our strength alone, we're blind. But Jesus, the Messiah, came to bring good news to the poor, release to the captives, and recovery of sight to the blind (Luke 4:16-18). He opens closed eyes, and brings new light, so we can see.

What opens your eyes? Have you ever tried to find your way in the dark? Did you hit anything? Have you ever discovered you were blind when you thought you could see? Was getting lost ever a good thing for you? What did you find? What did you see?

Free Cats

I once visited a New Orleans veterinarian who had a sign in his office window: "Free Cats." It was true. The waiting room of the office had a large container, like an aquarium without water, and inside were the free cats. Actually, they were kittens, maybe a dozen or so of them, and they were free for the taking. My first calico, Patch, came from there. We could have gotten more if we wanted. Take your pick of the litter.

But there are no free cats. A new cat from the vet needs shots and an exam. And, of course, once the new cat is home, there must be daily food and water and care. Only a very unworthy and irresponsible pet owner would neglect the free cat. A true owner will love the cat and take care of the cat. The cat is free but certainly not cheap.

The same is true for grace: it's free but not cheap. God's love for us is unconditional, and God's gift is not earned, manipulated, or forced. God loves us because of who God is, and who we are, just as we are. The relationship comes to us through God's initiative, but it invites our response. Grace comes to us freely, just as we are. But it will not leave us just as we were, if we accept it. God's love, like all love, invites us to give back. Love responds to love with love. Love makes us grateful stewards who offer ourselves generously. If we refuse to give back in love, we haven't really known the gift. We don't get it. But as we receive, we can respond more and more fully in love.

What is the gift you receive? What do you do with it? What does this gift demand from you? How does it change you? What will you give?

Saul in the Basket

Saul of Tarsus was a major threat to the early Christian church. He was educated strictly according to Jewish ancestral law, zealous for God, and a relentless persecutor of Christians. The Book of Acts recounts how he approved of the murder of Stephen and ravaged the church, entering house after house to drag Christians off to prison (Acts 7-8).

Christ encountered Saul while the zealot was on his way to Damascus to persecute the Christians. Christ asked: "Saul, Saul, why do you persecute me?" Saul was blinded by the brightness of the light that shone about him, and he obeyed the Lord's direction to go to Damascus, where he took the next steps of faith (Acts 22:5-11). Saul (later known as Paul) was healed of his blindness, was baptized and began proclaiming Jesus in the synagogues of Damascus.

It must not have been easy for Saul. He was a respected leader. He was well educated, forceful, articulate, and used to speaking for himself. He was a powerful man in his society. But his conversion was a radical change for him. As the Lord said, "I myself will show him how much he must suffer for the sake of my name" (Acts 9:16). Saul's encounter with Christ left him blinded and at the mercy of the people with him. His healing came at the hands of a stranger. His escape from Damascus required him to sneak out of town in darkness by being lowered in a basket, literally depending on his disciples who held him up and aided his escape. And he couldn't bring about his own acceptance into the community of disciples in Jerusalem. He had to keep his mouth shut while Barnabas told his story and persuaded the others to believe him. Saul would certainly

have been glad to use his own eloquence to convince them, but anything he said in that context would have seemed suspicious and self-serving. Again and again he found himself powerless, except in his ability to trust in Christ and trust others in Christ's name. The power of his life was beyond himself.

Sometimes we may discover our greatest personal strengths can become our most significant weaknesses. We may find ourselves blocked when we hang on to power, but we may be amazed by the possibilities available to us when we seem most helpless and vulnerable. We may find unexpected strength beyond ourselves as we let go of pretense and control. Like Saul, we may find healing, new direction, and acceptance in the hands of others.

How does it feel in Saul's basket? Does it tremble as friends lower it? Do you tremble in the basket? How does it feel to depend on others, and for them to depend on you?

Arc

An arc is a curved line segment. If an arc is extended far enough it will form a circle. The wider the arc, the longer it must extend to make a circle, and the more difficult it may be to imagine the circle it will become when the curved line is extended. An arc moves from one point to another without going through the space that's directly between the points. So an arc is less direct than a straight line in moving to a destination, but it avoids potential obstacles on the direct path between two points.

The Rev. Martin Luther King Jr. once quoted the abolitionist Theodore Parker, who said the arc of the moral universe is long, but it bends toward justice. Sometimes we need to move from one point to another, but a linear progression is impossible. The next step cannot simply follow the previous one along a straight path. It would be tempting to push straight ahead, but that's not possible or helpful. The real direction can be more subtle and changing along the way. It may be hard to see exactly where the path is leading because it involves a sequence of turns. The trajectory may be uncertain, with the final shape only visible to hindsight and reflection.

But the arc's curve can also be a kind of quantum leap. The arc moves over an intervening space or barrier to a new space, taking shape in ways that only become clear as the arc unfolds. Even when the direction of things is unclear, we can follow the arc to its completion and find its center.

What is the trajectory of your choices and actions? Where do they lead? What shape is your life taking? Are your choices moving your center? What forms the circle of your identity? What gets in the way? Does the arc carry you over the obstacles?

Lost and Found

Our greyhound Kiwi was found running loose in rural Kentucky. An abandoned greyhound is pretty unusual. Greyhound owners can be very protective of these dogs, and a missing greyhound can prompt all-out search parties. A farm boy found Kiwi beside a country road, and he thought she was a feral dog. She was scruffy, dirty, and underweight. Feral dogs kill farm animals, so the teenager pulled his truck over to the side of the road to shoot her. He reached into the back of his truck to get his gun. Then he felt a tug on his pants. It was Kiwi. She was nuzzling his leg. She wanted to be friends. So he put his gun back in the truck and invited her up into the truck cab with him. She was that close to being killed.

A few days later a friend brought Kiwi to us. We cleaned her up and gave her a home. Now she lives pretty well. I tell her she's our miracle dog.

Sometimes things can be so dark that we see no way out and no signs of hope. We're out of bright ideas, and we've exhausted our ingenuity. But the scene can change quickly, and we receive a second chance in life. Help can arrive in unexpected ways. Phillips Brooks, a nineteenth-century Episcopal priest and theologian, states in his sermon "New Starts in Life" that God never gives us any gift for its own sake, but so that we may know God through the gift. A discovered or rediscovered gift can be instrumental for sharing God's love. If we were lost, we may discover that we've been found.

Will you give others a second chance? When have you given or received a second chance, and how did it change you? When have you received unexpected help? What difference did it make in the situation—and for you?

Flying

Once when I was flying from Louisville to Tampa, I found myself sitting next to a woman and her mother, who was 95 years old and making her first flight. The mother was in the window seat and watching very carefully. We taxied to the runway, accelerated for a normal takeoff, and moved smoothly to cruising altitude. At some point, the older woman leaned toward her daughter and asked, "Why did we stop?"

It was a reasonable question. The scenery outside the window was changing quickly as we sped down the runway for takeoff, but the airborne view of sky, clouds, and ground was relatively the same. There was certainly a sense of motion as we gained airspeed on the runway, but (fortunately) the ride in the air was smooth. We were quickly gaining speed and elevation, but the perspective of our new altitude suggested otherwise. It was as if we weren't moving at all.

Sometimes we can be impatient with our lives when there seems to be no progress. The reality can be otherwise. It may be that much is happening and changing but in ways we can't detect. A seed may be growing in the ground for some time before a visible seedling emerges. Some prayers may be answered in ways we can't yet recognize. Unseen growth and resurrection life are suggested by John Macleod Campbell Crum's hymn text, "Now the green blade riseth from the buried grain" (*The Hymnal 1982*, #204), which says of the buried Jesus, "Laid in the earth like grain that sleeps unseen: Love is come again like wheat that springeth green." Even Jesus "slept unseen" in the time between the cross and his resurrection. On Holy Saturday we pray that we may await with

Jesus the coming of the third day, and "rise with him to newness of life" (*The Book of Common Prayer*, p. 283).

We may not recognize the signs of change in ourselves and around us as we engage our own ascending reality. New creation and possibilities may be unfolding in ways we can't detect. We may need to rest patiently, and wait, until we see how far and fast we've moved. At some point we may realize we're flying.

When have you waited for the first signs of a change? Were you impatient? What were the first signs of change to appear? Were you surprised when the signs of change appeared? What did you see? Did your perspective change?

Magnolias

My daughter, Claire, attended Converse College in Spartanburg, South Carolina, and the perimeter of her campus was lined with magnolia trees. I visited near the end of her senior year, and she told me that the magnolias drop their leaves when they bloom. There's nothing wrong with the magnolia leaves, but there comes a time for the tree to let them fall to the ground.

Sometimes we need to let go of something to engage our life and passion. The thing we let go may not be bad in itself. It may even be a good thing, but perhaps not the best thing for us at the time. To say yes to something may require saying no to any number of other things. Saying yes to an invitation of faith may mean saying no to some older patterns of behavior. Paying attention to the movement of grace may require saying no to attractive distractions that get in the way. Blooming can be a very costly process, when we drop our leaves.

Are you holding leaves that need to drop? What are they? Do you hesitate to let them go? Why? What happens when they drop? How do you feel without them?

The Cross

Christians encounter lots of cross images—in stained glass and on altars, on vestments and jewelry and steeples. These can be wonderful reminders for faith, but we can see them so often that we forget their meaning, and the cross becomes a decorative ornament or a trinket.

Let's be frank: the cross is an instrument of torture and death. Jesus died a horrible death on the cross. But the cross is also good news because it was the instrument of his self-offering and sacrifice. His resurrection brought the best out of the worst. The cross was Jesus' victory over sin and death. It provides the ultimate expression of God's love for us and our victory. The cross demands everything and makes everything available to us. It's how we drink the cup that Jesus drank and share his baptism (Matthew 20:22-23).

The cross is the place of intersection. Life and death come together at the cross, and life prevails. Sin and obedience come together at the cross, and obedience prevails. Hate and love come together at the cross, and love prevails. God's saving desire, intention, and action all come together in Jesus' sacrifice for us on the cross. Theologian William Porcher DuBose states in *The Ecumenical Councils*, published in 1897, that the cross is the way God lost and found himself in humanity and the way we lose and find ourselves in God.

At its most basic reality, the cross is just the intersection of two pieces of wood, one vertical and one horizontal. Living the way of the cross embraces the vertical and horizontal in our lives. Loving God "above" draws us into deeper relationship with others "below," as loving others can draw us to serve and know God more fully through them.

What's the cross in your life? Where does it appear? What intersects? How do you recognize the cross? Are you on it? How does it change you? How does it save you? What do you give?

The Stone

The Gospel of Mark records that Jesus' body was placed in a tomb after his death on the cross. The tomb was hewn out of rock and sealed with a very large stone against the door. Everything was final. Jesus' life was over. The grave was closed. There was the stone. It was so large that when Mary Magdalene, Mary, and Salome went to anoint his body on the Sunday after his death, they wondered who would roll the stone away for them. But when they arrived, they found it already rolled back, and Jesus' body was gone. A young man dressed in a white robe told them Jesus had been raised from the dead (Mark 15:46-16:6).

Sometimes on Good Friday we sing the hymn, "Were you there when they crucified my Lord?" (*The Hymnal 1982*, #172). The song asks, "Were you there when they nailed him to the tree?" "Were you there when they pierced him in the side?" And "Were you there when they laid him in the tomb?" Some versions of that hymn include a final verse that sings for Easter: "Were you there when they rolled away the stone?" It's a song of victory and new life.

The stone is not confined to Jesus and the tomb. The stone can be anything that threatens dead weight and finality in our own lives. The stone can be unbearable. The stone can be disappointment, loss, fear, unresolved grief, or deep sadness. The stone can drain all our energy and joy and leave us with a feeling of futility. But the stone isn't the end of Jesus or our hope. We rise with him, every day, and roll away the stone.

What is your stone? What does it look like? What does it obstruct? What happens when you try to move it? What helps?

The Opening Door

The disciples gathered in a house on the evening of the Sunday after Jesus' death, and they locked the doors (John 20:19). It was a reasonable precaution. They were known to be Jesus' closest followers, and he was brutally executed by the religious and political authorities. It was easy to foresee they would face the same brutal treatment, and they were afraid. The disciples were marked men in a very dangerous situation. They were hiding out. They were lying low.

I can imagine the disciples in the house, listening anxiously for sounds of an angry mob or approaching soldiers. But then the risen Jesus appears and stands among them. He wishes them peace. He shows them his hands and side and again wishes them peace. Then he sends them into the world, as the Father sent him. Jesus breathes on his disciples, giving them the Holy Spirit, and empowering them to forgive sins (John 20:19-23).

Never again do we see the disciples locking themselves in a room for fear of anyone. They receive the Holy Spirit from the risen Jesus, and they're sent with a mission. The world around them is absolutely as dangerous and threatening as before, but *they* are changed.

Inspired by the Holy Spirit, the disciples find the heart and courage to unlock the door and bring the gospel to the world. The disciples walk through an open door into a world of new possibilities, and the Holy Spirit is visible in their changed lives.

Do you feel the fear as you stand with the disciples in the locked room? What do you hear outside? What does Jesus offer you when he appears? Does the door open for you? Where do you go?

The Tipping Point

A beam balance provides very accurate measurements of weight by using a pivoted beam with weighing pans suspended from each of the beam's arms. An object is placed in one pan, and standard weights are added to the other pan until the two sides reach equilibrium. Fine corrections are made in precision balances by moving a slider weight on a graduated scale.

The point of balance is an essential starting point for discernment or helping another with discernment. Saint Ignatius of Loyola advises in the *Spiritual Exercises* that the person offering assistance "ought not to lean or incline in either direction but rather, while standing by like the pointer of a scale in equilibrium, to allow the Creator to deal immediately with the creature and the creature with its Creator and Lord." The tipping of the balance is the moment of decision in our lives. It's the turning point, the resolution of the crisis that hangs in the balance, or the decision that could go either way. It is addressing the question that my physician often asks when presented with a new condition to treat: "Is it getting better or getting worse?" Which way does the balance tip? Should the trend be encouraged to continue, or is an intervention needed? What do we hear when we listen?

We may consider a crisis to be necessarily a bad thing. We may associate a crisis with situations we'd greatly prefer to avoid—for example, a hostage crisis, a monetary crisis, or a health crisis. But crisis itself, like any turning point, is just a moment of discernment and decision. It's not bad or good in itself. It's the place where the path divides. Saying yes to one possibility may require saying no to other attractive options that we may weigh in the balance of our hearts and minds. A crisis can be a threshold for new life, or an occasion for decline and stagnation.

What's at the tipping point in your life? Do you face a decision? Are you at a crossroads? Where does each path seem to lead? What guidance do you find at the point of decision? Which road do you choose? How does the balance tip for you?

Hands

O ur hands distinguish us from other created animals. We don't have paws or claws. We have opposable thumbs, making it possible for human beings to write letters, paint landscapes, or perform brain surgery. A violin comes to life in the hands of an accomplished performer. In many ways, our hands represent our ability, our creativity, and our humanity. We may shake hands when we meet another person, thereby presenting ourselves for relationship. A person who can do many tasks of building and repairing is "handy." We offer our help when we "lend a hand." We "take our life in our hands" if we do something dangerous. We may "give a hand" by applauding at a concert or speech. We may "hold hands" with a loved one.

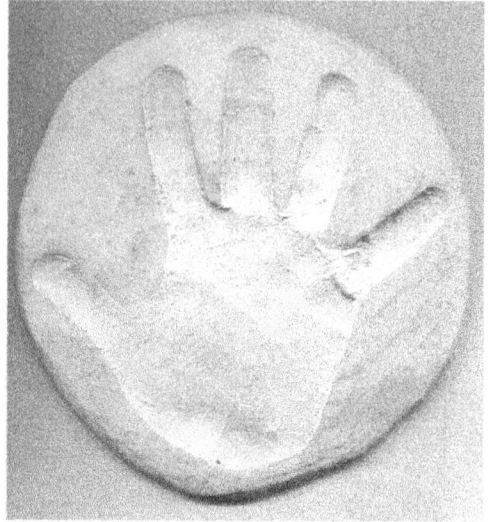

Hands also provide important ways to represent God's loving presence and our response. At an evening service of prayer called Compline, we commend our spirit into God's hands, and bless the Lord as we lift up our hands in the holy place (Psalm 134:2). Michelangelo's fresco for the Sistine Chapel depicts the hand of God nearly touching Adam's hand at the creation. The essential divine and the essential human draw near to each other, and new life is shared through their hands.

Jeremiah's description of the potter and the clay (18:1-11) provides an image for the interplay of God's initiative and human response. Austin Farrer, a priest and theologian in the Church of England, considers this image in his sermon, "The Potter's Clay," and reflects that God's hands are never idle in the creative process that saves us. As we respond or resist, God's hands are always present to work with us, inviting and shaping us. Our becoming reflects both divine action and human response. The divine agent contends and cooperates with the human agent. God's hands draw us beyond our resistance and inflexibility so we may be formed in creative, useful, and holy ways. It's the way of our completion. Farrer explains in his book *Said or Sung* that "the true life of the clay is to spin into symmetry under the maker's hand."

God's life works in our hands. The Rev. Alan Herbst, a priest who served at St. John's, Keokuk, Iowa, once preached a sermon on the hands of his parishioners—the worn, the rough, and the delicate—especially as he saw their hands when they opened to receive Communion. We may open our hands in love.

How does God touch your hands? How do you use your hands? What do you give with them, and what do you receive?

The Whiffle-Poose

One day my dad was in a playful mood and told about the "whiffle-poose," an imaginary bird that flies backwards. Because, he said with a twinkle in his eyes, the bird is more interested in where it's been than where it's going. The story was funny, but the problem is real. It's easy to see the "whiffle-poose" is flying blind and likely to crash. But it can be harder to know when we're stuck in the past.

The past can be tempting and comforting. We know how things worked, and didn't work, and we know our part of the story. Even the bad news is familiar and well worn. We know where we fit in and where things will lead. We even know the traps and pitfalls. But the future has no guarantees. Every opportunity has unknown dangers, and we just don't know what will happen next. We feel vulnerable because our usual barriers may be ineffective or gone. We must step into an unknown future, whichever way we go, and it's scary.

Greyhounds are sight hounds, which means that seeing is their primary sense for perceiving. Sometimes they just look away when they're spooked by what they see. They don't want to face it. That's what our greyhounds do if they see something like a scary cat when they're outside. Sometimes we are like the greyhound or the wiffle-poose, reluctant to face forward to see where we're going, and to look ahead to our destination. It can help to know that God will be present, even in an unknown future, and we can find our way. We can open our eyes to see where we're going.

What do you see when you look behind you? What do you see ahead? Have you avoided facing something you didn't want to see? What's your vision for the future? Where are you headed?

Bamboo

Bamboo is pervasive in Japanese culture both because of its beauty and utility. It can be used to make fences or flutes. An image of bamboo appears on the backdrop of the stage in traditional Noh musical drama. A gate usually made of bamboo demarcates spiritual and secular space in the tea ceremony.

Masao Takenaka, a Japanese Christian, states in *When the Bamboo Bends: Christ and Culture in Japan* that western symbols such as bread, grapes, and sheep often convey the Christian message, but these symbols are foreign to Japanese culture. Instead, Takenaka suggests, bamboo is a companion for daily life in Japan and an appropriate Christian symbol in Japanese culture.

Bamboo promotes spirituality in Japanese cultural life. The bamboo groves "invite a clean wind." This wind is pure and can be a reminder of the Holy Spirit. Bamboo is flexible. It bends under stress but doesn't break. It represents hope and resilience. It has strong roots and an empty center. The strong roots provide stability, and the empty center suggests humble self-emptiness before God. Bamboo represents a way of life that is open and resilient, flexible and durable, practical and beautiful.

Christ can be known in every culture, in the context of the culture's own images, symbols, customs, and patterns of life. It may be unhelpful to describe Christ as the "good shepherd" in a culture without sheep. Incarnational spirituality means that Christ is present and available to be found in the midst of everyday life, everywhere. Nothing has to be imported for Christ to be known. And so bamboo provides an excellent image for the flexibility, resiliency, and beauty of Christian life. In Japan—and elsewhere.

Does the bamboo bend in your hands? How can you use it? Is there a place for it in your home? Is there something else in your home (maybe something very ordinary) that is a symbol of your faith?

Sure Footing

A construction worker on a roof may need to step on a plank to get from one place to another. At some point, the worker makes a judgment about the plank. Will it hold his weight, or will it break and send him tumbling down? The worker's thoughts about the plank may be hypothetical as he considers his options. He must decide whether to expect the plank to hold, or not. But if he chooses to trust the plank, the decision is no longer abstract. He bets his life on the plank when he puts his weight on it. When the plank holds (and we hope it will!), the worker knows the truth of his decision—and the plank. This image is drawn from the theologian Austin Farrer, who also likens a faithful person to a mountain climber depending on the rope of an experienced mountaineer. The mountaineer's help is not fully engaged until the other climber's weight is on the rope. The relationship is most effective when the lower climber actually depends on the rope.

In a similar way, we may consider many interesting opinions about God and the meaning of faith. We can analyze and compare these ideas and discuss them with others. That's fine, but we won't know the truth of our theology until we invest ourselves. A would-be swimmer might read many books about swimming, but she can never begin to swim until she commits her body to the water and tests her strokes. Then she will begin to know the true value of her guides and manuals for swimming.

We must live faith—literally depending on God—to know faith. Faith can seek understanding and deepen with understanding. But faith is more than an idea, an understanding, or a school of thought. As William Porcher DuBose states in *The Soteriology of the New Testament*, the reality of Christianity is found in the actual salvation it brings. We can experience the reality of faith as we invest ourselves and trust our weight to God.

Jesus died on the cross for our salvation. He could have devoted that Friday afternoon to an interesting and helpful discussion of faith with his disciples, but he put his weight on the cross and trusted God. His resurrection was through the actual cross. We engage his new life as we commit ourselves through decision and action.

When do you depend on God? When do concepts of faith become real for you? How do you invest your life in God? Does this shape how you know God, and your understanding of faith? How does your commitment make a difference?

Turning Around

I was an undergraduate intern in the psychology department of a hospital in Nashville. One day the clinical director went to give some important tests to a patient, and he took along a graduate student and me. We were serious about the significant task ahead and moved quickly through the hospital. We passed a patient who was sitting on the floor near an elevator. He was wearing a patient's brown uniform. He turned his head slowly, painfully, side to side. His eyes were half closed, and he seemed to wince. All three of us passed by him on our way to the appointment. The director turned around to see what was wrong, and we followed him back. The clinical psychologist almost knelt before the patient to face him, and asked, "Are you hearing voices?" No, the patient had been through some kind of oral surgery, and he was in considerable pain. There was blood in his mouth.

I must admit I wasn't going to stop for the patient. We had important work, and I would have kept going. I was busy and needed to be someplace. I was in a hurry. At least someone turned around. Someone saw the need that was right before our eyes, and I followed. That was my conversion.

New directions may appear in surprising times and ways. Unimagined possibilities and opportunities can present themselves to us. But we need to be listening with our hearts, observant, ready to respond, ready to delay or release our plans and agendas. Our real mission may be something unexpected that's right in front of us.

Do you hurry past the patient as he sits on the floor, or do you turn around? When have you been surprised by another's unexpected need? When is your routine a distraction from what you need to see?

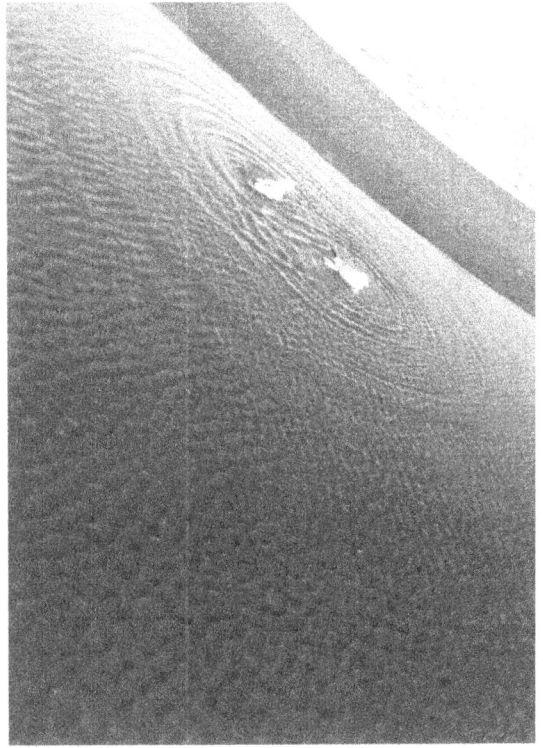

Fire

The day of Pentecost was punctuated by tongues of fire that rested on the disciples (Acts 2:3), and even today we describe the Spirit's life and our faith in terms of fire. We pray that God may "kindle our hearts, and awaken hope" and we ask that we may "burn with heavenly desires" (*The Book of Common Prayer*, pages 124, 285). We seek the presence of the Holy Spirit who is "comfort, life, and fire of love" (*The Hymnal 1982*, #504).

Fire can be a surprising image for faith. Fire can be threatening and burns can be horrible. But fire has a basic place in human lives and history. Fire was critical in the first steps of human civilization, providing security against predators, warmth for cold places, and light for dark times. Fire was at the heart of cooked meals and gatherings of family and friends, the earliest forms of society. Even today we may find our most basic needs are served by fire. If we cook or heat with gas, we find a pilot light that burns for us. When we drive a car, we turn the ignition key to spark a controlled burn that propels us.

But fire is beyond us, never really owned or controlled by us. Like the wind, fire shifts and moves in ways we can't predict. It's not ours. I can't recall a dispute over ownership of fire (unlike land or water rights). Maybe that's because fire can be shared without diminishment—like love. If my torch is lit, I can share its fire with another torch and both can burn brightly. Sharing the fire doesn't diminish me or my fire. At the Easter Vigil, the new fire lights the Paschal Candle, which brings light to a dark church. The light of Christ spreads to everyone present, so many new lights are born from the one fire. The new fire, the light of Christ, is exalted and not diminished as it spreads. God's fire burns brightly when we give it away.

Are you on fire with God's love? How do you share the light of Christ and the fire of God's love? How do you know this fire? When has it made a difference for you?

The Saxophone

My son, Jacob, is a jazz musician who plays the baritone sax. The "bari" is a large saxophone, and it sounds when he blows through the mouthpiece and fills the instrument with his breath. Then he plays the keys and creates amazing music. But no matter how skillfully he plays the keys, the music stops if his breath stops. His breath is in the music and makes it possible.

In a similar way, God's life is in us first. God chooses us before we can choose to obey or cooperate with God. Before we can seek to know God or discern the divine will, God is already with us. In Christ, all things hold together (Colossians 1:17). Without God's presence, the music of our lives would just stop. We would not be. God's initiative makes our initiative possible. We can say yes to God because God continues to say yes to us.

God's creation isn't done. Creation isn't a completed one-time event. It unfolds in us and all that exists. Our life begins with God and continues through God's presence. As Julian of Norwich states in *Revelations of Divine Love*, God is nearer to us than we are to our own soul. We may play the keys of our life with all our skill, but each sound begins with the breath of God.

Can you feel God's presence in a breath? Inhaling, what do you receive as your lungs fill with air? Exhaling, what do you give back, what do you offer, what do you share?

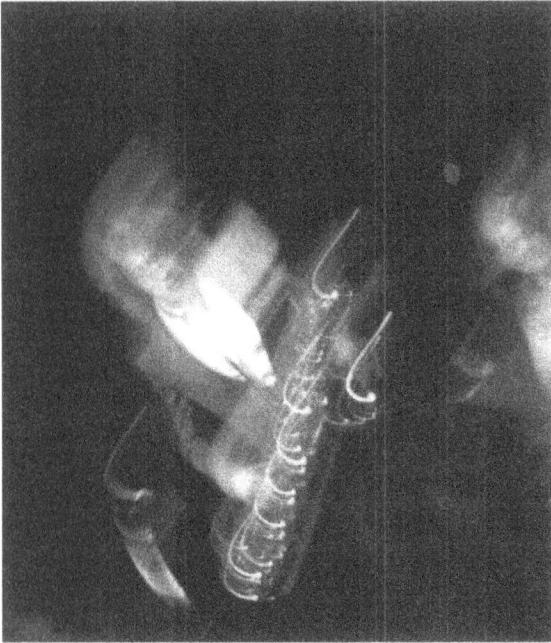

On the Way

Two of Jesus' disciples were walking to Emmaus on the day of the resurrection, and they met an unexpected companion who joined them. The disciples were sad, talking about everything that happened when their Lord died, and at first they didn't recognize Jesus. As they walked, he interpreted the things that were said about him in the scriptures. It was late in the day as they approached the village, and the disciples persuaded him to stay. They recognized him as they shared bread (Luke 24:13-31).

The road can be a challenging place. Even if we don't encounter bandits or highwaymen, we may lose our way and get lost. We may miss our connection and find ourselves stranded. Our luggage may fly away to an unexpected destination. We may wonder where to find needed services or even the next exit. The road can be threatening and disorienting. It can also be tiring and filled with inconveniences. The unknown may be more than we bargained for when we started. On the road we face our need.

But the road can be a place of discovery as well as vulnerability. Edward Schillebeeckx, a Dominican and theologian, states that the Dutch word for experience, *ervaren*, means to travel in the country. Our experiences on the road can transform us.

Jesus finds the disciples on the way, between their point of origin and their destination. There is nothing expected about this encounter. He approaches them in their sadness, as they try to make sense out of the bad things that just happened. It's appropriate that they meet as dusk approaches, so they stand literally between light

and darkness. In these gathering shadows, Jesus reveals the meaning of the scriptures and his suffering. He discloses himself to them. Their hearts burn within them as they talk with him on the way (Luke 24:32).

Our travels make it possible for us to step into something new. We may be separated from our typical routines and defenses and find ourselves suddenly available to new people and situations. We may find our Lord meets us in the dusky places of our life to reveal himself to us. If the experience of the journey makes a difference, we'll be new people when we arrive. We should be on the way.

Have you been changed by a journey? Did something unexpected happen? What did you find on the way? What did you see? What obstacles did you encounter? What did you discover about yourself? How did you change?

The Second Hug

Every weekday my wife Victoria leaves for work before I do, and I see her off as she leaves the house. I give her a hug and close the garage door when she leaves. One morning, I gave her a second hug. For no special reason, we lingered together for just a few minutes before she left. Later that morning, she used her cell phone to call from the road to say she was stuck in traffic. There was a major collision on the highway just ahead of her on the way to work. Ambulances were taking people to the hospital, and tow trucks were moving the wrecked cars. Given her speed and the timing of the accident, I figured she missed the collision by just a minute or two—perhaps the time it took for a second hug. I promised to always, always give her a second hug. Of course, there's no telling what happens to any of us in a given day, and there's no way to predict whether a moment's delay will protect or endanger. We're vulnerable creatures who live in a world of risks. We can hope, pray, and trust when our loved ones are away from us and out of our sight.

A faculty colleague of mine is from Nigeria, and he tells me that in his native Nigerian language there's no word for "love." The nearest statement to "love" in his language is an expression about seeing the loved one always. It would literally be something more like "I have my eyes on you," but really means that I see you wherever I go. You're "in my eyes." Of course, the people of his homeland are not lacking affection—on the contrary. But love is more to be lived out than spoken directly.

Loving someone, we go with them even when we're apart, whether in safety or danger. Loving others, we see them wherever we turn and find countless reminders of their presence with us. Loving someone, we find ways to express our love in everything we do. We might send a message or place a call, we might prepare a gift to share, or we might just carry them in the thoughts and moments of our day. In many ways we have them with us, in our eyes and hearts, as in the communion of God's love.

We don't see God in a direct sort of way, as if we were watching an exotic creature in a cage at the zoo. But we can have God in our eyes. We can see God in others, and in the world around us, wherever we go.

Who is "in your eyes"? Where do you see them? How are you connected when apart? How do you know God is present in your life? How do you know God through others?

The Rudderless Ark

Noah built an ark in response to God's warning of coming destruction and promise of a covenant. When the rains came and the flood rose high above the earth, the ark "floated on the face of the waters" (Genesis 7:18). The ark on the waters is recalled in a contemporary prayer, ascribed to Alan Jones, a former dean of Grace Cathedral in San Francisco: "In your hands we rest/ In the cup of whose hands sailed an ark/ Rudderless, without mast.// In your hands we rest/ Who was to make of the aimless wandering of the Ark/ A new beginning for the world."

Noah was anything but passive in the face of the coming threat and God's saving invitation. He listened carefully and worked hard. He built the ark to exact specifications—300 cubits long, 50 cubits wide, 30 cubits high. He made it of cypress wood, covered inside and out with pitch, with three decks, a roof, and a door in its side. He diligently followed all God's instructions. Then the flood came, and he entered the rudderless ark. He didn't need a compass, a sail, a map, or a rudder. He had no destination in a world covered with water and no timetable in a storm that probably seemed endless.

Noah let go of control when he entered the ark as the flood began. After working hard with his own hands, he surrendered his life to God's hands. There was surely much to do in the ark, but in a deeper sense it was a time of rest for Noah and everyone in the ark. It was a time of waiting and watching until the flood ended, and God's purposes came clear. As the flood continued and the rains fell, it would have been easy to worry that God had abandoned him in his time of need. He might have cried out "my God, my God, why have you forsaken me?" (Psalm 22:1), as Jesus did from the cross. But God remembered Noah and all the creatures on the ark. The rains finally stopped, and the waters eventually abated. Noah, his family, and the creatures left the ark to make "a new beginning for the world," and God blessed them to "be fruitful and multiply." This new beginning was possible because Noah wandered in the rudderless ark. He was willing to work, risk, and wait.

Inside the ark, do you feel impatient or trapped? Do you wonder how long this flood will last? Do you want to escape? When have you done everything possible, and then had to wait and trust in God? What happened while you waited? How did you know the time for waiting was over? Was there a new beginning?

Newborn

When my daughter Rebecca was born, I cut the umbilical cord and immediately held her in my arms. "I love you, Rebecca," I said. "I love you." This was before she learned to say a word, or played drums in the high school marching band, or was elected to Phi Beta Kappa in college. This was before she chipped a baby tooth running away from the big girls at church, or went to the high school prom with her first boyfriend, or learned to speak Spanish. She just was. And I was there with her, and I loved her.

Unconditional love can seem so impossible. There must be a catch. As if we must really have to prove something, earn a prize, close a deal, or figure it out. But God's love is just there for us. God really loves us. Before anything we do, or say, or plan. And even after some of the things we've done, and said, and planned. God loves us, unconditionally, tenderly, like a newborn in a parent's arms.

Jesus says we must receive the kingdom of heaven like a little child (Mark 10:15). Our availability and openness is essential to participating in the life and love of God. The little baby in my arms was totally available to help and totally open to receive what she needed to receive. She had no hidden motives or calculated agendas. She was just there to love and be loved. And as she loved, she grew.

The limiting factor in the divine-human relationship is us. We can only give and receive so much, and we fall short of the glory of God (Romans 3:23). At times we may be stingy, irritable, self-centered, or distracted. Our human limitations cause all kinds of obstacles in relationships, and we may even hurt the people we love the most. We may be slow to reconcile and less than generous. But there's no limit to God's love, or God's invitation for us to draw nearer and be healed. Sometimes we may be rather strongly defended against the love of God, along with the changes that God invites. The adventure of faith may seem like a precarious movement into the unknown, but it is new birth, surrounded by God's love.

How does it feel to hold the newborn child? How do you experience new life? What do you give and receive?

Sunrise

The new day begins with glory when sunlight fills the clouds and the eastern horizon. Golden light breaks the darkness like a crack in the dome of the sky. Homer recalls the shining of dawn's "rose-red fingers" in *The Odyssey*. Jacob Boehme, a seventeenth-century mystic, describes the sunrise in terms of "the morning-redness." It's the color of new life and hope and the promise of a new day visible in majestic skies. The color of dawn may be orange or red. Perhaps you can see the sunrise in the reddish-orange ink used by William Blake, an English poet and painter, in his illuminated printing, with dawn's light breaking into every word.

The sunrise says to wake up. Roosters crow. The world is stirring. People get out of bed and stand up. We "come into the daylight's splendor" (*The Hymnal 1982*, #339). Look up! The Buddha answered, "I am awake!" when asked, "what are you?" Being awake is living in the present moment, right now, without distractions or buffers. Being awake is living in a new day. The possibilities come alive in each moment.

I once visited a cemetery in Spartanburg, South Carolina, where the graves were positioned to face east. They face the horizon of each new morning, waiting to rise in glory in the first light of that final day. At the opening of Morning Prayer, we say, "Lord, open our lips. And our mouths shall proclaim your praise." We can see God's bright glory in the morning and praise the giver of light. We're awake!

What wakes you up? What does the morning bring for you? What is today's gift? Where's the light? What's on the horizon? Are you ready?

The Broom

We can sweep a floor to the glory of God, said George Herbert, a seventeenth-century Anglican priest. God can be seen in all things, with all tasks done for God. The work then becomes an expression of faith, and no burden. Devotion transforms both the sweeping and the one who sweeps. It makes "the action fine" (*The Hymnal 1982*, #592).

God finds us, and we find God, through the things of this world. God is present in creation and works through it. We find God in the details and everyday contexts of our lives. Saint Benedict states in his *Rule* that the vessels of the kitchen are as holy as the vessels of the altar. We can know God through the events and things of everyday life. The infinite God is not beyond our world or our most basic needs.

God's love is particular, tangible, and available in the midst of the situations we face. We can place our hands in God's hands so the divine generosity, love, and forgiveness are known through us. Our actions can then reflect both God's invitation and our choice. We may be amazed to discover we're most ourselves when our choices most fully reflect God's will. Austin Farrer calls this "double agency," and it's visible in the cooperation of the divine and human agents in a shared expression of love. We can know God present and active in our lives as we work with a computer, a paintbrush, or a broom.

How does the broom feel in your hands? Can it be an instrument of faith for you? When do you find God through a task or job? How does faith make a difference for your work?

The Beautiful Desert

The afternoon before a half marathon near Tucson, Arizona, Victoria and I found ourselves on the same airplane with other runners who would be in the race with us. "It's a boring course," one of the runners warned us. "You just run on a highway for mile after mile through the desert. There's nothing out there. It's just empty." Well, I thought, it's always good to know the course before you run it.

The sky was dark and cloudless when we arrived the next morning, but a full moon made the desert surroundings easy to see. The moonlight reflected off large stones or rocks that stood out across the road from where we stood. Tall cacti sprung from the fields, and acacia trees provided a scraggly break to the open landscape.

The sun was rising by the time the race started, and it grew higher and larger in the sky as the miles went by. The predawn chill was gone, and the day got warmer. We ran through a valley with an irregular ridge of mountains around the desert perimeter and much open space in the foregound. The course went along the straight line of the highway until we approached the outside of the city. At one intersection, a hawk was perched on a traffic signal, maybe watching the procession of runners on their way to the finish line.

The desert wasn't empty or boring. It was beautiful. It was filled with contrasts and surprises. It was alive. The perspective changed with every step, and I didn't want to miss any of them. There was so much to see. It was a different world.

The Gospel of Matthew (28:16-17) records that after the resurrection, the disciples "went to Galilee, to the mountain to which Jesus had directed them. When they saw him, they worshiped him; but some doubted." Some saw the risen Jesus and worshiped him, but others didn't believe when they saw him. That's how things went throughout his earthly ministry. Not everyone who met Jesus became a believer, and some who didn't believe in him became aggressive enemies, ready to kill him. It was as if they saw with different eyes.

As the poet T. S. Eliot says, we can have the experience but miss the meaning. We need to "see" with our heart and understanding as well as with our eyes, or the perspective will be faulty. Some could only see a carpenter's son when they saw Jesus. And some only saw empty space when they visited the desert.

What do you see in the desert? What is the desert for you? Have you seen something amazing in an unexpected place? Did you wonder how you missed it before? Did anything help you see?

Tobacco Juice

I once visited a building that housed a convent in Nashville, Tennessee, and part of the building was known as the "tobacco juice floor." It appeared that one day the Little Sisters of the Poor went to the Nashville railway yards to seek contributions. A sister approached an engineer in a locomotive, and she held up her hand seeking alms for the poor. The engineer didn't respond well to her appeal, and he filled her open hand with tobacco juice. The sister calmly wiped off her palm on her habit, and said, "That was for me. Now what do you have for God's poor?" The engineer offered nothing at that moment, but some time later he found the sisters' convent and brought them a gift. Actually, it was a lot of money, enough money to build a new floor of the convent. The tobacco juice floor.

Rejection feels bad. That's what happened when the sister held up her hand for an offering. The engineer rejected her request in a way that was personal, demeaning, and repulsive. But she didn't take it personally, or rather, she distinguished herself from what he did and opened the door for something better. Instead of responding with an insult or storming away, she held her ground. She was true to her mission. She calmly repeated her request for a donation to help the poor. She gave him another chance. And if it took him awhile to act on it, he accepted her invitation with generosity. He finally gave what she asked, and much more. It was his redemption and probably meant more to her than a new floor in her building.

At one time or another we may find ourselves lost and needing to be found. This situation is recalled by John Newton's hymn text "Amazing Grace" (*The Hymnal 1982*, #671), which famously exclaims, "I once was lost but now am found, was blind but now I see." But this very moving hymn can suggest that being found by God when lost is a one-time event. It doesn't work that way. Whatever our best intentions, our life will include times of making mistakes, falling short of the glory of God (Romans 3:23), and getting lost. The Episcopal marriage service includes a prayer that the couple will seek each other's forgiveness and God's forgiveness "*when* they hurt each other" (*The Book of Common Prayer*, p. 429, emphasis added). The possibility that they will never hurt each other is not considered. There are no perfect husbands, no perfect wives, no perfect relatives or friends or co-workers, no perfect parishioners or clergy, no perfect students or teachers.

The good news is not that God somehow makes us perfect people on earth. And we certainly don't need to make ourselves perfect to "qualify" for God's love. The good news is that God finds us when we're lost, opening the door for healing, forgiveness, and new hope. God's forgiveness is infinite, and we're called to follow the example, forgiving others "seventy-seven times" (Matthew 18:22), in limitless ways. The invitation of God's forgiveness often appears in the hands of another person.

The charitable and patient sister gave the engineer a chance for redemption and generosity. Instead of turning away from him, she held out her hand. Again.

Have you given or received a second chance? Have you been rejected, and tried again? Have you rejected someone, and later changed your mind? Have you reconciled with an enemy, or someone you hurt? How?

The Eighteenth Camel

There was once a wealthy man who lived in the desert with his three sons. The man owned seventeen camels when he died. His sons were dismayed and confused when they read his will, which left half the camels to the oldest son, a third of the camels to the next oldest son, and a ninth of the camels to the youngest son. They couldn't agree on what to do. The numbers didn't work for them, and they began to fight. Finally a wandering sage came along on a camel, and he offered a solution for their dilemma. He added his camel to the father's estate, and that changed everything. Suddenly the broken pieces fit together nicely. When there were eighteen camels, it was easy for the oldest son to take his half with nine. The next son easily took his third with six camels. And the youngest son took his ninth of the camels with two. That left one camel unclaimed, the sage's camel, and he rode away on it.

The sage came from outside the situation, and his gift allowed the conflict to be resolved in a good way. Then he removed himself (and his camel) when they were no longer needed. He was never entangled in the conflict. He didn't hesitate to get involved, and he didn't linger when his job was done.

Jesus warns his would-be disciples that "foxes have holes and birds of the air have nests; but the Son of Man has nowhere to lay his head" (Luke 9:57-58). He became deeply and lovingly involved with the people he served, but he moved from place to place throughout his ministry. He never owned a home, never opened an office, and never settled in one place. He moved quite freely until his last days in Jerusalem. He made a difference for many people in a variety of situations. He healed the sick, proclaimed good news, and raised the dead. Sometimes his presence was an occasion for reconciliation and forgiveness. Like the sage with the eighteenth camel, he offered what he had in a way that changed everything. He helped things to fit and heal, and then moved on, taking nothing for himself.

When have you been able to "loan" yourself, and then take yourself back? How did you offer yourself? What difference did you make? Did you avoid entanglements? Have you ever left a situation too early, or stayed too long? Are you ready to help, and ready to leave?

Rabid

One summer I was working for the security police at Vanderbilt University, and I heard a startling report from the radio dispatcher. There was a rabid dog loose in the university hospital! I quickly went to the hospital floor and ward where the mad dog was supposed to be. There was a crowd of people gathered around the exit, looking with great concern through a small window in the door.

On the landing of the stairwell was a hound. He was sitting quietly and panting heavily in the warm (not air conditioned) hospital stairwell. It was summer in Nashville. The dog was drooling. And hot. He looked up at me sweetly through the window.

"I'm not going out there with that dog," said a burly security policeman. "Step back," I said, and opened the door to the stairwell. The hound seemed pleased with my company and unaware of the ruckus he was causing beyond the door. "Come on, boy," I said, whistling for him and snapping my fingers. "Let's get out of here." So I skipped to the steps, and he followed me down some eight flights of stairs, with a little encouragement along the way. Finally we reached the ground floor. I opened the exit door, and the hound sauntered out of the hospital. I called in the "mission completed" code to the radio dispatcher. It was fun. And I'm glad I got there first. Someone might have hurt him.

The people on the other side of the door were judging by appearances. They thought the hound was foaming at the mouth. They jumped to a conclusion and started to panic. I expect none of them had ever seen a rabid dog, but they were being vigilant.

Appearances can fool us. It may be tempting to reach conclusions on the basis of race or age or gender or ancestry. But we're easily misled by prejudices, assumptions, and stereotypes. The latest gossip can also bias us and keep us from ever really knowing the person before us. The accuracy of an unfair judgment is not improved by many repetitions. We may need to wait on a decision, despite the apparent clarity of appearances. Everyone seemed to agree the hound was rabid, but he was just hot and wet.

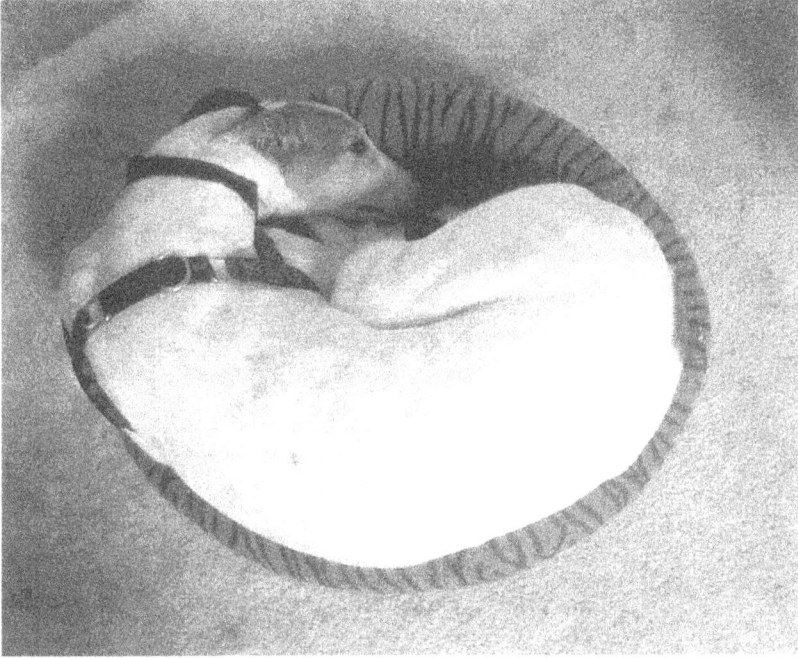

Imagine you're an outcast. How do people react when they see you? Do they touch you? Have you been judged wrongly on the basis of your appearance? Have you been categorized unfairly? Has a prejudice or stereotype prevented you from really seeing the person in front of you?

Homeward Bound

Homecomings are not always easy. When Jesus returns to his own hometown and teaches in the synagogue on the sabbath, he encounters hostility (Mark 6:1-6; Luke 4:16-30). The people think they know who he is (and isn't) because they know his family. In Mark's narrative, the people ask, "Is not this the carpenter, the son of Mary and brother of James and Joses and Judas and Simon, and are not his sisters here with us?" They take offense at Jesus, and he's amazed by their unbelief. Their attitude is so bad that Jesus can do no deed of power in his hometown, except heal a few sick people. He states, "Prophets are not without honor, except in their hometown and among their own kin, and in their own house." In Luke's account of this scene, the people become enraged at Jesus and want to throw him off a cliff near the town. Fortunately, he passes through the midst of them and goes on his way. It's not an easy homecoming.

Thomas Wolfe, author of the novel *Look Homeward, Angel*, is well-known for saying "you can't go home again." He's right. The buildings and even the people of a former home may be there, but "home" may be gone. The actual place may be very different from the remembered home. People returning from time overseas may experience "reverse culture shock" when the old place they find isn't the home they remember. Life has gone on without them. Things have changed. People and relationships have changed. The place is different. They're different.

The Rev. Debra Trakel once mentioned at St. James Episcopal Church, Milwaukee, that the expression "hobo" is a contraction of the phrase "homeward bound." The expression was first applied to soldiers returning from the American Civil War. We can hope that homeless people, and all "hobos," will reach their destination and find a good home.

In a larger sense, we're all to be "homeward bound." Our true home is not just a memory. We may or may not be able to return easily to our hometown, or the place we now call home, but we all should be trying to find our way home. The completion of this home is ahead of us, in the completion of our lives in God's hands. God is our sanctuary, our oasis, our refuge, our greatest adventure, our security, our home. As in John Newton's hymn text, "Amazing grace" (*The Hymnal 1982*, #671), "tis grace that brought me safe thus far, and grace will lead me home." In God we find our homecoming.

What do you miss when you're away from home? What reminds you of home? Does anything make it difficult for you to go home? What gets in the way? How do you find your way home? Who welcomes you? Does anyone interfere? How do you know you're home?

The Missed Start

I once missed the start of a half marathon. It was silly. I was late getting to the start but thought the race was delayed. Lots of runners were standing around, but they were waiting for another event. My race had already started, and I was upset when I realized what happened. A race director was helpful and said I could follow the race emblems painted on the street at the intersections to navigate the course. I started by myself. There was computer chip timing, so my official finishing time would be whatever I ran. The timing system beeped when I crossed the start, and I began looking for my lost race.

Fortunately for me, there was lots of help. Someone painted all those race emblems on the course, and the way was clearly marked. Otherwise, I would have been wandering through downtown South Bend, Indiana, on an early Saturday morning. At one point I passed a policeman and asked him about my lost race. He smiled and said I was going the right way. By the time I started catching up with the back of the pack of walkers and runners, there were people along the way to cheer and offer support. I was back in the race.

Did you ever miss a race? If not an actual race, were you missing when it mattered for your marriage, or family, or work? Were they all gone when you finally arrived? Did you find yourself on the outside when you expected to be in the middle of things? Did life go on without you? Whatever the causes or reasons, there can still be time, and a way back, with others to help on the way. Like the prodigal son whose father celebrates his homecoming after many disappointments (Luke 15), we can be glad when others welcome our return with open arms.

When did you find yourself unexpectedly on the outside of things? What did you miss? Could you find your way back? Who helped? How did you return?

A Smile

Victoria and I were in a crowded line of disembarking passengers on a jet. It seemed like everybody was standing in the aisle after we unbuckled our seat belts, but no one could move to get off the plane. Things were tight, and I was ready to get out of there and on our way. I was surrounded by bags and elbows. But Victoria noticed the little girl ahead of us was wearing new shoes with sparkling colors. "Oh, you have such pretty shoes," she said to her, and the girl smiled. It was an incredible smile that filled the girl's whole face and lingered for several moments. Everything seemed to brighten. It was fun. Being stuck in a crowded plane was fun. She had new shoes.

God finds us where we are, and hope appears in unexpected ways. It's usually the extraordinary in the ordinary, and we may be surprised by an unplanned encounter with love that changes everything. It just sneaks in, and we see things differently. The occasion can be something small, like a gesture of courtesy, a special gift, a word of encouragement, or a little girl's smile.

How do you feel in the crowded line of passengers on the plane? What difference does a smile make? Were you ever trapped in a situation? Did something help? How did you see the situation differently?

Silhouette

I once ran a half marathon in Austin, Texas, and the race began at dawn. After a mile or so, the course turned due east, facing a magnificent sunrise. It was a clear day, the large sun was low and round on the horizon, and the light was dazzling. The sunrise was glorious. The procession of runners filled the road with fast movement, and the line of them extended ahead as far as I could see. The light put the whole field of runners into silhouette, so it seemed like one large and very busy creature (with many legs) as we all ran forward. There was enough light to distinguish some details of the shape and form of each runner. But the impression of the whole field of runners was stronger than the details of any individual. It was a single silhouette, a single pattern with many moving parts. Some of the runners would prove to be faster or slower than the others, but we were all running in the same beautiful light. We were all in the same race. Our connection was visible in the dazzling sunrise and in the silhouette.

Sometimes we may live as if we're totally unrelated to anyone else. We call our own shots, make our own way, and let others do the same. But we're not just running a lonely race of our own. We're connected.

What do you see in the silhouette of the crowd? Where are you? How are you connected with others? How do you maintain your individuality when you're with them?

The Dance

Edward Schillebeecky recounts in his book *Jesus* a story told by Martin Buber, a Jewish philosopher who died in 1965. Buber told of a crippled man who stood to describe the great Baalschem, a holy sage who would leap and dance as he prayed. The crippled man was so carried away in his telling of the story that he "had to show how the master had done it, and started to caper about and dance." He was cured! Buber concludes, "That is how stories should be told."

The crippled man telling the story of the dancing sage did more than provide a collection of facts, a bit of history, or an entertaining description. He made the story *dance*. He became the story, and it lived in him. The story of the dancing Baalschem became his own story, his dance. It picked him up and moved him. Some Christians might say the Spirit was on him. It left him different, healed, a new person. It danced him. That's why we read the gospel and tell the stories of Jesus. We get caught up in his dance. He will move and turn us in surprising ways to share his life.

We act ourselves into being. If we love, we become lovers. If we play, we become players. If we work, we become workers. If we cheat, we become cheaters. Every day we shape who we are. So it's never too late for change and new hope, and that's good news. A Chinese saying advises never to close the book on a

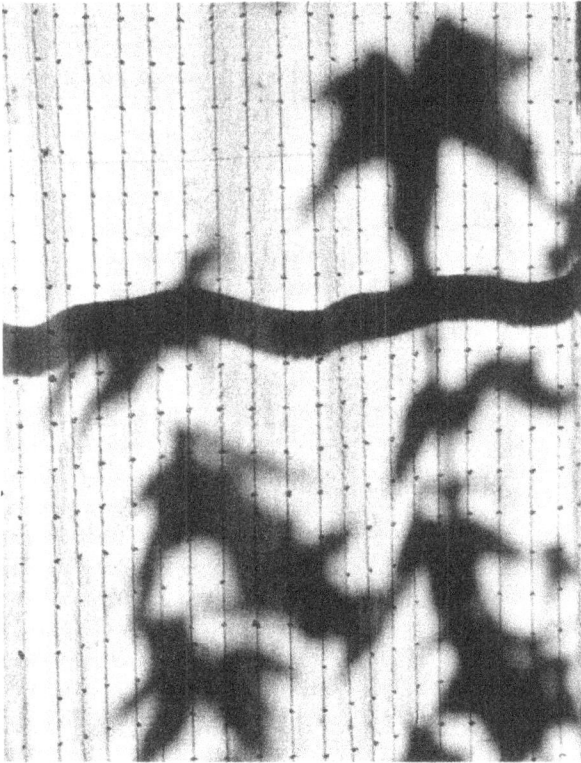

life until the coffin is sealed. It's never too late. We can find and be found by new possibilities, any day. We can be moved by a story. We can dance!

What is dancing in your life? Has a healing story ever come to life in you? How are today's decisions shaping your new life?

Two Copper Coins

The widow put two small copper coins into the temple treasury. Her gift was pretty small in comparison to the large sums donated by the rich people, but Jesus praised her gift. She gave more, Jesus said, because she gave everything she had to live on, while the others gave from their abundance (Mark 12:41-44).

The Rev. Edwin Conly once preached at St. Andrew's Episcopal Church in Nashville, Tennessee, that the value of a gift is seen in the heart of the giver, not the gift itself. The widow dropped a meager two copper coins into the temple treasury, and it probably didn't seem like much. But, Jesus explained, she gave everything, all she had. It was an incredibly generous offering from her. The rich would return to their remaining riches, but the widow sacrificed everything.

Despite the widow's extreme generosity, we don't know her name. "Sine Nomine," "Without Name," is the title of Ralph Vaughan Williams' famous tune for the hymn "For All the Saints" (*The Hymnal 1982*, #287). It fits well with the reading from Ecclesiasticus (44:1-10, 13-14) for All Saints' Day, which sings the praises of famous ancestors, and then recalls: "but of others there is no memory; they have perished as though they had never existed." They died without name. And yet they were godly people "whose righteous deeds have not been forgotten."

The widow's name is lost to us, but we remember her generosity. We also may never be mentioned by name in histories or memorials, but we can give what we have and know our name in Christ.

What's your offering? Have you made or received an anonymous gift? What difference did it make for the one who gave it—and the one who received it? What did it mean to you?

The Zeon

The Eastern Orthodox eucharistic liturgy includes a moment after the breaking of bread when the deacon pours a few drops of hot water into the chalice of wine. This is the zeon. The term is from the Greek for "boiling," and it's also known as "living water." It's an ancient practice that symbolizes the warmth of faith and the descent of the Holy Spirit. Like anything sacramental, the zeon is an outward and visible sign of an inward and spiritual grace. The zeon is a sign of the Spirit, who brings Christ's real presence into the eucharistic elements and our lives.

The Spirit's presence is "living water" for us, providing many gifts and a world of new possibilities. The turbulence of the Spirit wakes us up and breaks us out of comfortable old patterns and tired ways of doing things. The fire of the Spirit warms our hearts and sends us with mission. The power of the Spirit guides us around or through obstacles that seem impossible to overcome. The Spirit inspires our best efforts and invites our full response in love. The Spirit draws out our gifts and brings us together in faith.

The words of the ancient hymn *Veni Sancte Spiritus* (translated by John Mason Neale), known as the "Golden Sequence," suggest the loving action of the Holy Spirit in our lives: "what is rigid, gently bend; what is frozen, warmly tend; strengthen what goes erringly." The miracles of the Spirit are not always sudden. The fire of the Spirit warms us but does not burn us. The Spirit

encourages us to set aside defenses that obstruct God's love. This may take awhile but rushing won't help. I'm told the most perfect crystals form most slowly. The Spirit warms us patiently and courteously, without violence, so our hearts may gently awaken to life. The drops of warm water at the zeon will not boil over or scorch. The zeon brings the Spirit's warmth and energy to the chalice, and us.

When has God warmed you with help and inspiration? How did this make a difference for you? Was there a change in your life?

Window

Icons have been described as windows onto heaven. During the controversies over icons in the seventh and eighth centuries, icons were misunderstood to be idols. But icons are not to be worshiped. The icon serves to engage the vision and life of the worshiper, who may then "see through" the image to the sacred reality it depicts. The icon points beyond itself to something more—a spiritual reality that's not contained by paint or wood. Richard Niebuhr, a famous twentieth-century theologian, said that a cultural expression may point beyond itself to Christ, as the soaring architecture of a cathedral lifts a visitor's eyes heavenward, and as Thomas Aquinas found Aristotle's philosophy to point beyond itself to divine glory. There are many windows onto heaven.

We can discover the extraordinary in the ordinary, as the everyday things of our world can reveal God's transcendent presence in our midst. God finds us, and we find God, through the circumstances and materials of our lives. This is an incarnational spirituality. Paint on wood can reveal the Savior to our senses. We may perceive God's presence in apparent coincidences, the beauty of nature, or the ordering of creation. God is always present to us, and there are many ways to perceive and recall God's presence in our lives.

We need a window to see beyond our own room. But we can take windows for granted. When we see a beautiful view, we may only appreciate the vista before us and not the window that gives the perspective. We may only notice the window if it's smudged or cracked, and our view is impaired. The view itself is beyond us, but we can do our best to keep the window clean and unobstructed.

What are your windows onto heaven? What do you see through them? Is there a vista? How do you see through ordinary things in life to God?

Zumba!

One day at my health club, I heard really loud music, clapping, and much shouting in a large studio room. It was the Zumba class, and maybe thirty people were dancing and exercising their way around the room in a wild circle of energy. It was a hip-swaying, elbow-pumping, loud-whooping, fast-stepping parade. They were alive. They were happy. They were jumping. They were fun. They were moving like people with something to celebrate.

King David certainly knew how to celebrate. When he brought the ark of God to Jerusalem, he "danced before the Lord with all his might." David and the whole house of Israel presented the ark with shouting and the sound of the trumpet. But Michal, a wife of David, looked out the window and saw him "leaping and dancing before the Lord," and despised him. She thought David was vulgar and criticized him for acting shamelessly before the "the eyes of his servants' maids, as any vulgar fellow might shamelessly uncover himself!" (2 Samuel 6:20). But David was undaunted by her criticism. He danced before the Lord and knew the people would honor him (2 Samuel 6:12-21).

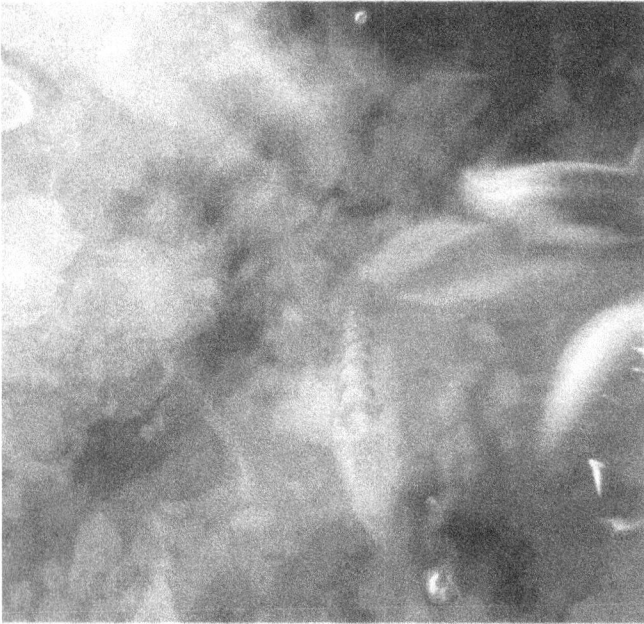

Unfortunately, I have seen Christian worship that was more in the spirit of Michal than of David. When I was a child, my family attended a church that was rather reserved. This was a time when unconfirmed children were not allowed to receive Communion. I remember watching the adults return to their pews from the altar. Their expressions tended to be fixed, somber, even grim, as if they just completed a necessary but somewhat unpleasant task. I didn't know what they were giving those people at the altar, but I figured it must taste really bad!

The rules for receiving Communion have changed since the days of my childhood, but we can still lose sight of common prayer as a time to celebrate God's love. We have good news. We have much to celebrate. Lord, open our lips. Lord, move us!

Is your prayer a celebration? Is your celebration a prayer? Can you dance it? What moves you?

The Bad Wolf

When my daughter Claire was about four, she had a really scary nightmare. It may have been prompted by the gas furnace outside her door that came on with a bang in the middle of the night. She dreamed a giant wolf was tearing through the wall of her room and coming to get her! She screamed bloody murder. I was amazed that a child so small could make a sound so large and chilling and piercing. It was pure fear, a life or death fear, and it was everywhere, filling everything, leaving room for nothing else.

Claire was in terror when I reached her. Of course, it wasn't nearly enough to reason with her, to show the evidence and prove there was no wolf in the room, or in the closet, or under the bed. There was no wolf coming through the wall, or even in the yard, or anywhere in the neighborhood. There was no wolf, no wolf. She was afraid and not about to be talked out of it.

The fear made it hard for Claire to sleep in the following days. The wolf was still with her. It took a few days, but we finally chased the bad wolf from Claire's room. I held her hand, and she tightly held mine, and we went looking for the wolf, several times a day. We'd knock on pieces of furniture in the room to scare him out. We'd check the closet and under the bed. We'd tell him to *go away*! These were our wolf hunts. Finally she laughed, and the wolf was gone.

Fear is easier to face when there's a hand to hold. Fear is easier to face with love. Fear can paralyze, but it can be broken with a laugh.

One of the most frequently repeated commands in the Scripture is "fear not." Jesus tells his followers not to fear those who can do nothing worse than kill the body (Luke 12:4). He tells his disciples not to be anxious about persecution or worry about what to say when called before the authorities for the sake of the gospel (Matthew 10:18-19). He urges his disciples not to be anxious about food or clothing (Luke 12:22-27). When the angel Gabriel appears to Mary at the Annunciation, and again when an angel of the Lord appears to the shepherds to announce Jesus' birth, they offer assurance: "Do not be afraid" (Luke 1:30, 2:10). After Jesus' resurrection, an angel says to the women, "Do not be afraid." They quickly leave the tomb to tell the disciples about the resurrection, and then encounter Jesus himself, who says to them, "Do not be afraid" (Matthew 28:1-10). Fear no evil, not even in the valley of the shadow of death (Psalm 23). As we let go of fear and anxious self-concern, we can begin to trust and share the faith we're called to live.

When were you afraid? What scared you? How did fear shape the way you saw things? What could you do about the fear? What broke the fear? Did anyone help? Have you ever helped a frightened person? How?

First Steps

The Gospel of Mark records that Jesus saw Simon and Andrew fishing as he walked by the Sea of Galilee. Jesus invited them to follow him and "fish for people" (1:16-20). They immediately left their nets and followed him. Jesus went a little farther and saw two more fishermen, James and John. The brothers were mending their nets in a boat. Immediately Jesus called them, and they followed him. They became disciples. They left their father Zebedee in the boat with the hired men. He must have been shocked as he watched them go! The disciples stepped away from their homes, their families and friends, their livelihood and family business. Where would they go? Where would they stay? How would they support themselves? What would happen to them? They couldn't know.

Jesus called the disciples to follow, and they were together with him. That's all they really knew. Jesus asked without hesitation, and they responded immediately. They got out of the boat. They invested themselves and stepped into an unknown future, sacrificing their way of life and just about everything. As the famous twentieth-century theologian, Dietrich Bonhoeffer, states in *The Cost of Discipleship*, it was costly grace (not cheap grace) "when Peter left his nets and his craft and followed Jesus at his word."

A child making her first steps may hesitate and stumble, but it's the beginning of a new way of life. I have seen some first steps, and they're amazing to witness. The first steps can be the hardest, but there's a new world to explore, and the next steps can be easier. As stated in the *Tao Te Ching*, a classic sixth-century Chinese text, a journey of a thousand miles begins with a single step. We all start somewhere as we take the first steps of a new beginning. It can be a journey of discovery and surprise.

When have you taken first steps? Did you hesitate? Did you falter? Where did your steps take you? What did you discover? Where do your next steps lead?

The Windmill

I once drove past a large open field in Indiana and was surprised to see it converted to a wind farm. A row of large windmills (actually wind turbines) extended as far as I could see, and their blades were spinning in the wind like a squadron of giant airplanes. I'm told these windmills provide clean energy.

Of course, the wind "blows where it chooses," as Jesus says to Nicodeums (John 3:8), meaning the Spirit and everyone born of the Spirit. We cannot know "where the wind comes from, or where it goes." But we can recognize patterns in the wind's frequent movements and be ready to respond. We can locate a good place for a windmill.

God moves very freely, but grace consistently reveals divine love and fulfills God's promises. We can count on God. Before his death, Jesus promises his disciples that he will not leave them comfortless or orphaned. He will come to them. As the Gospel of John recounts, they will live because he lives (14:18-19). At the Last Supper, Jesus identifies the bread and wine with his body and blood and urges his disciples to share this meal in remembrance of him (1 Corinthians 11:23-26). We continue to find him really present in Communion, and whenever two or three are gathered in his name (Matthew 18:20). These are dependable promises,

and they invite our response. Grace moves us to choose in faith, but we must choose. We can locate ourselves where the wind blows.

Yves Congar, a Dominican born in 1904, offers an image for his theological and scholarly vocation in the General Introduction to *I Believe in the Holy Spirit*: He will "sing his own song, like an Aeolian harp whose strings will vibrate and sing with the breath of God. He will "stretch and tune" his strings with the "austere task of research" so the Spirit can "make them sing a clear and tuneful song of prayer and life." Grace brings our gifts to life, but we must do our part. We can let the wind turn us. We can make ourselves available. We can tune our strings and welcome the breath of God.

Do you feel the wind? How does the wind of God's love move and turn you? Does it surprise you? Can you tune your strings to play God's tune? What do you hear?

Thanksgiving

One year my parish had a special Thanksgiving celebration. The food offering for the poor was arranged in front of the altar, and the church was decorated with harvest symbols. This was to celebrate Thanksgiving Day, a national holiday recalling days of thanksgiving prayers by seventeenth-century colonists in Massachusetts and Virginia. Thanksgiving Day is also a major holy day in the Episcopal Prayer Book and a time to give thanks to God for the fruits of the earth and the labors of the harvest. In the words of Henry Alford's Thanksgiving hymn, we "raise the song of harvest home: all is safely gathered in, ere the winter storms begin" (*The Hymnal 1982*, #290).

Thanksgiving is a way of Christian living, not just a day. We offer thanks to God for everything we've received. We take nothing for granted. We don't claim all the credit for our success or assume it's our due. We recognize others and thank them. Thanksgiving points us beyond self-centeredness and arrogance. Thanksgiving acknowledges that life and its opportunities are gifts from God: "It is he that made us, and we are his; we are his people, and the sheep of his pasture" (Psalm 100:3). A lack of thanksgiving can indicate a lack of belief in God. In Islam, ungratefulness is understood in terms of sinful disbelief (*kufr*).

Every Eucharist expresses our thanksgiving to God for all we have received. Eucharist means thanksgiving, and the eucharistic liturgy of the table is "The Great Thanksgiving" (*The Book of Common Prayer*, p. 361). In thanks, we offer bread to be blessed, broken, and shared. We offer ourselves in the same way. In thanks, we appreciate others and express gratitude to them. They matter to us, their gifts make a difference, and we tell them. We see beyond ourselves, and give beyond ourselves, with thanks.

What gift do you offer in thanks? Who receives it? How do you offer it? Why are you thankful? Who will you thank?

The Book Left Behind

It was a Bible. A retired priest gave it to me before I went to seminary. I used it in a class and put special tabs on it before my ordination exams. But I left it behind when I moved from a parish where I served for about ten years. It was in the library, and I forgot it.

Years later, a parishioner was looking for a study Bible, and the priest invited her to take one from the library. She picked the Bible I left behind and appreciated my markings and notes in it. After awhile, she realized it was my Bible and sent it to me with thanks. I was amazed. It all came back to me with that well-worn Bible: my friend's gift, the times of study, the good years of ministry in that parish, and the many good friends. And even if all the times weren't good, it was a reminder of something important that was never really left behind. It was an unexpected gift and a blessing. Something gracious returned to me.

I'm reminded of a favorite scene of mine in the movie version of J. K. Rowling's *Harry Potter and the Order of the Phoenix*. Luna Lovegood (looking for her missing belongings) tells Harry that her mom "always said the things we lose have a way of coming back to us in the end. If not always in the way we expect." Or, as Rumi, a Persian Muslim mystic of the thirteenth-century, says in *Unmarked Boxes*, "Don't grieve. Anything you lose comes round in another form. The child weaned from mother's milk now drinks wine and honey mixed."

The gifts we offer can become gifts we receive. We reap what we sow (Galatians 6:7). Some people say, "what goes around comes around," and we do seem to shape our destiny by our actions, as some Eastern religions describe in terms of karma. Jesus advises in the Sermon on the Plain that we'll not be judged if we stop judging; we'll not be condemned if we don't condemn; we'll be forgiven if we forgive; and if we give, we'll receive generously. Indeed, "a good measure, pressed down, shaken together, running over" will be lavished upon us, because the measure we give will be the measure we receive (Luke 6:37-38). Our expressions of generosity, courtesy, forgiveness, and compassion may encourage others to respond and live in similar ways.

As the famous Indian peace activist Mahatma Gandhi said, we can be the change we want to see in the world. Aware or unaware of what they're doing, and for better or worse, people may follow our lead. The world will be a quieter place if we're gentle and a more frightening place if we're cruel. A sharp accusation can prompt an angry defense, and a smile can draw out a friendly response. We can begin to shape our culture and society. As we give ourselves, we may discover we're living in a world of abundance and find unexpected ways to offer and receive. The Bible I received became a gift for a stranger and eventually returned to me with thanks as another gift.

Has something lost ever returned to you in an unexpected way? Have you been surprised by a gift you received, or an unexpected opportunity to offer a gift? Has a situation in your life ever changed because of a gift you gave or received? What was the gift? What difference did it make?

The Ringing Bell

The Rule of Saint Benedict directs that monks will immediately set aside what they're doing when the signal (such as a ringing bell) is given for daily community prayers. They will respond "with all speed" so nothing is "preferred to the Work of God." The moment the bell rings is the time for response without hesitation or delay. When the bell rings, a monk who's writing shouldn't linger to dot an "i" or cross a "t" before putting down the pen and leaving immediately for the next moment of encounter with God. That's obedience. As David Steindl-Rast, OSB, states in *A Listening Heart*, "the really important thing is that in a monastery we do things not when we feel like it, but when it is time."

This discipline is rooted in belief that God is available to us in the everyday moments of life, and we participate in God's presence by responding with our hearts, best energy, and focus. Without delay. If this is the time to know and be known by God in the prayers of the community (or work, or a meal, or service, or anything else), there's nothing more important to do. A yoga teacher of mine once said "there's no better place for you at this moment than here." It's only in the present moment that God comes to us, and we can engage God by being present to our current reality. Our meeting God will be in a present moment, like now, and never in a time or place without us.

Procrastination can be really harmful because the moment of God's encounter can be missed. We can buffer ourselves from God. If we procrastinate, we can be less than fully open to God's next gift to us. We can miss the opportunity. There will be other times to encounter God in the future, but each present moment is precious and not to be wasted. Our commitment is to be here, really here, to find and be found by God.

We can listen for God, even when God's presence is not heralded by a bell or any sound. We can be alert for unexpected opportunities and coincidences, the synchronous moments of life. We can listen to others with our hearts as well as our ears, and be available without delay or distractions. We can be attentive. We can be present where we are, and listen for God. That's why the first word of Benedict's *Rule* is "Listen." We can know God in all the moments of our lives, clearly, like a ringing bell.

Do you "hear" God? Can you find God in your life? Do you listen to others? Do you listen for God? Are you attentive? Are you ready to respond? What distracts you?

Christmas Trees
and Chocolate Cake

In 1914 the German and allied armies were entrenched on the western front of Europe as Christmas drew near. It was the first Christmas of the first world war. Conditions were miserable, icy, and muddy. The armies were stalemated. Their trenches were in shouting distance of each other, sometimes within thirty to seventy yards. The lines were separated by entanglements of barbed wire and a narrow "no man's land" that was a killing field.

But something amazing happened that Christmas. The soldiers along the lines made their own truce. They quit killing each other for Christmas. The initiative came from the soldiers in the trenches, not the generals or national leaders. The truce began near Ypres, Belgium, on Christmas Eve. The German soldiers held up Christmas trees with lights. At first the allies were suspicious and thought the lights could indicate an attack. The Germans sang "Silent Night" ("*Stille nacht, heilige nacht*"). Eventually soldiers on both sides laid down their weapons and stepped into "no man's land." The truce was spontaneous and spread along much of the five hundred miles of the western front. Thousands participated.

The truce began differently in different places, so there are many accounts. The Germans took the initiative. In one place, according to Stanley Weintraub's book, *Silent Night*, signboards appeared with the message "You no fight—We no fight." In another place, they invited their adversaries to meet them halfway across "no man's land." In one place, the singing of carols became almost antiphonal between the opposing lines. The British sang "The First Noel," and the Germans sang "O Tannenbaum."

In one place, the Germans had already laid a foundation for the Christmas truce. A few days before Christmas, they lobbed a carefully wrapped chocolate cake into the British trenches, inviting their enemies to share a one-hour cease fire that night to celebrate their captain's birthday. The British stopped firing and applauded when a German band played

"Happy Birthday." The Germans tossed a chocolate cake (instead of grenades) at their enemies and offered a truce.

After the truce began, the soldiers met in the middle of the killing field. They were friendly. They exchanged food, drink, tobacco, and personal items such as photographs, buttons, and badges. They played soccer, using steel helmets to mark the goals. One soccer game ended when the ball landed in the barbed wire and deflated. The soldiers sang

carols and made toasts. They recovered and buried the dead, and there were even a few joint funeral services for the fallen on both sides. In some places the truce was just for a day, but in other places, the truce lasted for several weeks. The allied troops had been exposed to propaganda that described the German soldiers as barbarians. But they found their enemies to be very much like themselves, with much in common.

A theology student of mine once made a class presentation on the 1914 Christmas Truce, and he brought a chocolate cake to share with everyone. We should all eat that cake.

Can you help to start the Christmas truce? Have you ever ventured into the empty place between hostile groups? Have you helped to stop a conflict with an enemy or a friend? Have you made a peace offering to someone who was angry at you? What can you offer your enemies?

Fully Clothed and in his Right Mind

The sick man was wild and strange. He lived beyond the edge of town, where people in cities put their trash and their dead. He went naked for a long time. Instead of living in a house, he lived among the tombs. Sometimes he was bound with chains and fetters or kept under guard for safety's sake. But nothing made a difference. He always broke away. He was tortured by an unclean spirit or demon, and it drove him into the wild. It drove him wild, and nothing helped. Until he met Jesus. At first he cried out and fell at Jesus' feet, shouting, "What do you want with me, Jesus, son of the Most High God?" But Jesus delivered him from the unclean spirit and healed him. After his healing, the people from the town found him at Jesus' feet, fully clothed and in his right mind.

Perhaps the strangest part of the story follows the man's healing. When people from the town saw him healed, they were afraid. "Then all the people of the surrounding country of the Gerasenes asked Jesus to leave them; for they were seized with great fear." Instead of celebrating the man's amazing healing, and the one who healed him, they were terrified. The healed man begged to go with Jesus, but Jesus sent him home to "declare how much God has done for you" (Luke 8:26-39).

Change can be difficult, even when it's change for the better. Engaging change may require new ways of thinking and being. It may require letting go of prejudices and preconceived notions. Until the time of his healing, the man's place in society was clear. He was on the fringes, an outcast, someone different from others in behavior and appearance. No one took him seriously, except as a possible threat.

But everything changed when Jesus healed him. He was able to rejoin society. He could live in a home, have a job, share life with friends and family. If others would let him. They would need to change their attitudes to welcome him back. They would need to see him in new ways. They would need to relate to him differently and let him find a place with them. He might want to live near their homes, take a job in their workplace, or marry one of their daughters. Many adjustments would be needed. It was a challenging situation that would demand a lot of work. There was much that couldn't be explained or predicted in advance.

It's no surprise the healed man wanted to go with Jesus instead of staying in the town. Jesus healed him, and the people were less than inviting. The man still frightened them, even though he was healed. But Jesus urged him to stay in the place where he belonged and tell the story of his healing. His community can be transformed by this good news. They can discover its meaning and blessing. He will no longer be an outcast, and the people can overcome their fears. They can change together.

How do we exclude people from our communities? What are the barriers that keep people out? What do we fear? When have you changed your attitude toward another person? When have you hoped another person would see changes in you?

The Dog's Cry

It was Saint Francis Day and the blessing of the pets at St. Raphael's parish in Lexington, Kentucky. Most of the parishioners brought dogs to bless, and one brought a beagle. She entrusted her beagle to a friend when she went to run an errand, but the beagle didn't like that. He did what beagles do so well. He cried mournfully and loudly for her return. AW-ROO! AW-ROO! AW-ROO! Even though his person was some distance away, I'm sure she heard him.

This reminded me of the poem "Love Dogs" by Rumi, a Sufi (Islamic) mystic. In this poem he describes a simple man of prayer who encounters a cynic. The cynic challenges his practice of prayer, asking if he ever heard back any response to his prayers. The man admits he has not and ceases his prayers. But then Khidr, a guide of souls, comes to him in a dream and suggests the image of the dog's cry for its master. Khidr explains, "This longing you express is the return message." The cry itself is its own response and expression of the bond of relationship, as a yearning prayer is itself union with God. "There are love dogs no one knows the names of," Rumi says, "give your life to be one of them."

The desire to pray is itself a prayer. The seeking of union with God is itself an expression of that union. God's grace precedes and upholds our prayer. God in us prays to God for union with God in us. Our cry to God is God crying out through us for the love of God that God will provide. With God's grace, we may go beyond our human limitations. Shortly after the Transfiguration, a man asked Jesus to heal his son if Jesus could. When Jesus challenged the man's lack of belief, he exclaimed, "I believe, help my unbelief!" Prayer and fulfillment are deeply connected as Jesus grants the father's request to heal his son (Mark 9:14-27).

Jesus urges us to ask and promises we'll receive; he urges us to seek and promises we'll find; he urges us to knock and promises the door will open (Luke 11:9-12). Like the beagle who yearns and cries for his master, our intent to share God's love expresses the sharing of God's love. Even the cry of separation is an expression of union. Our cry to God is God's cry in us and union with God who hears us.

When do you cry for God? How do you reach out for God? How do you know God is present? How does God find you?

Show your love today, Lord.

Help us listen for you. Be present.

Let us breathe in your love.

Let us find you everywhere.

Help us soar in your sky.

Help us touch your heart.

Show your bright glory.

Open our eyes so we may see.

Open our hearts so we may love.

Open our hands so we may serve.

Show your love today, Lord.

— RBS

About the Author

Robert Boak Slocum is the author, editor, or co-editor of eleven books. He serves as dean of the School of Arts & Sciences and a professor at St. Catharine College in Kentucky. He served congregations in the dioceses of Louisiana, Milwaukee, and Lexington. He received his doctorate in theology at Marquette University and taught as a lecturer and visiting assistant professor in the Theology Department at Marquette. He was the president of the Society of Anglican and Lutheran Theologians, and the co-convener of the Society for the Study of Anglicanism. He was ecumenical officer for the Diocese of Lexington, and he serves on the board of the *Anglican Theological Review*. He lives in Danville, Kentucky, with his wife, Victoria, and many rescued greyhounds and cats. He has three grown children, Claire, Rebecca, and Jacob.

Acknowledgements

Thanks to all who helped this project, especially Victoria Slocum and Rick Bate, who helped to prepare the images. Also thanks to Rebecca Slocum, Bob Cooper, Fred Himmerich, and Ashok Bedi for editorial suggestions. And thanks to Richelle Thompson, Carole Miller, and the entire Forward Movement staff.